ALL THINGS SPIDERS FOR KIDS

FILLED WITH PLENTY OF FACTS, PHOTOS, AND FUN TO LEARN ALL ABOUT SPIDERS

ANIMAL READS

WWW.ANIMALREADS.COM

THIS BOOK BELONGS TO...

_____

_____

WWW.ANIMALREADS.COM

CONTENTS

Welcome to the wonderful world of spiders! — 1
What Is a Spider? — 7
The Different Species of Spiders — 11
The Fascinating History of Spiders — 41
Where Do Spiders Like to Live? — 47
Unique Characteristics and Appearance of Spiders — 51
The Life Cycle of Spiders — 61
Thank You! — 69

WELCOME TO THE WONDERFUL WORLD OF SPIDERS!

Few animals on our planet can stir up strong emotions in people like spiders can. The critters that people love to hate, spiders are among the most incredible animals on our planet. Clever, resourceful, hardworking, and beneficial to us humans, spiders have suffered a bad reputation for years.

But all that's about to change...

Welcome to the wonderful world of spiders!

Spiders are some of the hardest-working creatures in the animal kingdom. In many forests, gardens, farms, and homes, they are the most important biological tool for pest control. This means that, rather than spray crops and gardens with harmful and polluting chemicals, we can rely on spiders to keep our crops and forests in tip-top shape.

Spiders feed on pesky pests that have the potential to ruin crops and kill plants and other animals. This keeps our farming lands healthy. Much like bees, which pollinate the plants we need to survive, spiders allow us to cultivate land so we can eat and be healthy.

Now isn't that a lovely thing to do?!

It is no surprise that spiders have a lot of fans around the world. Many scientists dedicate their lives to breeding and studying them, hoping to learn more about everything that makes them so unique.

Unfortunately, there are also some people who are afraid of spiders because a few can be dangerous to us humans if we are bitten by them.

However, if you are an animal lover, you already know that all animals need is our respect, and plenty of space to roam around. Learning about the different species of spiders and how to identify the dangerous ones keeps everyone healthy – **both spiders and people!**

Ready to learn more about the incredible and awe-inspiring spider?

What are you waiting for?!

Let's go!

WHAT IS A SPIDER?

A lot of people mistakenly think that spiders are insects, but they actually belong to an animal class called **arachnid**, which also includes scorpions, mites, and ticks. *What do all these creatures have in common?*

Well, they have **legs with multiple joints and no skeleton on the *inside* of their bodies** – *like you and I do.* The outside of an arachnid, the flexible yet hard shell, is actually the external skeleton.

Know what that's called? An **exoskeleton**, of course!

Arachnids also have special 'add-on extras' like claws, stingers, antennas, wings, or unique jaws that help the animal chomp down on its food. You might consider this the arachnid's special superpower if you will.

What are the spider's superpowers, you wonder?

We bet you might know what these are!

Spiders have **sharp fangs** that may (*or may not*) contain **venom**, which is a toxin that is injected into you, rather than a poison, which is a toxin swallowed by you. They also have what we call **spinnerets**, an extraordinary organ that allows the spider to 'spin' its web.

Spider webs are one of nature's most fascinating and amazing creations, and we are so excited to share all we know about them in this book.

WHY DO SPIDERS SPIN WEBS?

Because they can't knit!

THE DIFFERENT SPECIES OF SPIDERS

We hope you are sitting comfortably as you read these lines because we have a lot of super exciting spider facts to share with you.

Did you know that, so far, biologists have discovered about **45,000 different species of spiders** in the world? These incredible creatures can adapt to all sorts of climates and landscapes and live almost everywhere on earth. *The only places you won't find spiders?* Those would be the peaks of the highest mountains (*too cold and windy!*), the two polar regions (*that's the North and South poles*), and the world's oceans.

Interestingly, some spiders can actually swim, yet they still prefer to live in small bodies of water like ponds and lakes. The raft spider, for example, can even run on the water's surface.

But first... from the most common and impressive to the largest, the smallest, the most dangerous, and the outright cutest spiders in the world?

Let's go ahead and meet them all!

THE COMMON HOUSE SPIDER (AKA AMERICAN HOUSE SPIDER)

As the name implies, this is the most common spider species living in homes across North America today. If you see cobwebs on your house's walls or roof, you are assured to be sharing your living space with an adorable and very common house spider.

These tiny little critters measure about a quarter of an inch in length, taking up no space at all in family homes. In return for free lodging, these clever creatures keep homes free of mosquitos, ants, fleas, and flies. So, fear not, dear friend, common house spiders are just the kind of '*uninvited guest*' you'd be wise to keep!

Although common house spiders do have venom, it is not harmful to humans.

THE BLACK WIDOW

Now here is a common house spider that you ought to know. The Black Widow is the second-most common spider living in US homes and the reason over 2,500 people visit poison centers in the US each and every year.

Here's what you should know about one of the most venomous spiders of all.

Black Widows can be dangerous if threatened, but, luckily, they don't actually like to live *in* our homes. **They'd much prefer the garden!** This spider makes its home in plants, burrows, and large woodpiles. In fact, most people are accidentally bitten when they stick their hands in and around their gardens, without knowing they are disturbing a Black Widow's home!

The Black Widow is not one of the most poisonous spiders in the world, but it is the most venomous in North America. By comparison, the venom of this spider is about 15 times stronger than that of a rattlesnake. Although a snake can release much more venom in one bite than a spider can so, technically, it isn't nearly as dangerous to fully-grown humans.

Children living in areas where Black Widows are present should be taught to be very careful when pottering around their front or backyards, lest they inadvertently disturb the nesting site of a Black Widow.

Female Black Widows are black and shiny, with fiery red markings on their bellies. They are usually about four times larger than males. Males are a lighter color with pink or red spots.

Many people might not know that there are many species of Black Widow spiders. In the US, there are three species of Black Widow spiders (northern, southern, and western). While South

America has two distinct species and one each in Australia and New Zealand.

FUN FACT: *How did the Black Widow get its terrifying name?* Because female Black Widows are known to eat their male partners!

SOUTH AMERICAN GOLIATH BIRD EATER TARANTULA

The flamboyant show-offs of the spider world, tarantulas, are one of the best-known spider species in the world. How could anyone not notice them?! Tarantulas are big, hairy, and some say even a little bit scary. But never fear! Tarantulas are some of the most laid-back spiders in their animal kingdom. Their venom is not very powerful at all, although, truth be told, **a bite can hurt quite a bit.**

Still, like all spiders, tarantulas only bite if they feel threatened, so as long as you treat them with care and kindness, you can even get quite close to them. **Provided you are in the company of a spider expert, that is.**

Tarantulas are unique because of their size and hairy disposition, so they belong to a spider family all their own. All up, there are over 1,000 different types of tarantulas in the world.

It is no surprise, then, to learn that the largest spider in the world is a tarantula. Specifically, a species called the Goliath bird eater tarantula. We agree that the name alone is enough to send chills down our spines.

A GOLIATH spider that can EAT BIRDS??!

Goodness...

The Goliath bird eater is **SO** big that it can easily take up an adult human's entire hand or cover the entire forearm of a small child. **Gulp!** Its body can reach over 5 inches in length and weigh about 6 ounces. *Those hairy legs?* **They can grow to about one foot in length!**

The Goliath of the spider-world lives in the northern countries of South America, so you might be lucky enough to spot one if you tour the Amazon Rainforest.

FUN FACT: Goliath doesn't actually feed on birds, although it *could* if it wanted to. Instead, it feeds on ground-dwelling insects, mice, frogs, snakes, and lizards. This mammoth spider has an amazing line of defense against predators: not only is its bite strong enough to break through the skull of a small animal like a mouse, but it can also release little irritating hairs that cause severe itching. These little hairs are on their abdomen, and when threatened, the Goliath will furiously rub its belly with its back legs to release them. *Cool, right?*

THE BROWN RECLUSE

Much like the Black Widow, the Brown Recluse is known for being highly venomous, although rarely do bites cause serious complications for humans.

The Brown Recluse has a small, light-brown body and long, spindly, dark-brown legs. It's easily identified because it has a violin-string pattern on its light-colored back.

Another common spidery house guest in North America, the Brown Recluse, is most active between March and October – a period known as Brown Recluse Season in affected regions of the continent.

The venom of this spider is so powerful that it can destroy blood vessels on the site where it bites, and the wound can easily get infected. Luckily, when humans get to the hospital super quickly, they can get the medication they need to heal. Unfortunately, there is no **antivenom** for a Brown Recluse spider bite, but we do have plenty of medication to combat any infection.

FUN FACT: Antivenom is a medication that counteracts the effects of an animal's venom. That's why it's called *anti* (against) venom. How is antivenom made, you wonder? This is the cool part! Venom is extracted from a poisonous animal and injected into a large animal (*usually a sheep or horse, but don't worry, it's a tiny amount that doesn't hurt them*). The animal will then start to produce antibodies to fight the venom, and that's the antibodies scientists extract to produce antivenom for humans!

SPINY ORB-WEAVER

One of more than 70 spiders renowned for their incredible spikes, the spiny orb weaver is an absolutely stunning spider. It might look like the kind of spider you wouldn't want to mess with, yet, in reality, it is totally harmless. Their body can be white, yellow, or black, and they usually have black polka dots and six pointy spines along the edge. Females are much more colorful than males, but either way, this prickly little creature is instantly recognizable.

The spiny orb-weave usually weighs about 6 ounces and is only half an inch long. It produces one of the most beautiful webs there is, measuring over 12 inches across. This beautiful spider is an awesome pest controller, and many farmers will purposely keep some in their barns to keep moths, flies, mosquitos, and bees at bay.

THE GIANT HUNTSMAN

The spider with the largest leg span of all is the adored giant huntsman, one of Australia's most iconic creatures. **Its legs can span a width of an entire foot – the size of a dinner plate!**

So why is this enormous creature so adored? Because this gentle giant will live a quiet and happy life on the corner of your ceiling, feasting away on flies and mosquitos while being no bother to you at all. Australians are pretty accustomed to living with huntsmen – the country is home to almost 100 endemic species of spiders that are found nowhere else on earth.

FUN FACT: Named after its hunting technique, the huntsman doesn't waste its precious energy building a web to trap prey. Instead, it will stalk its prey and wait until the last possible moment before lunging forward at breakneck speed and catching it on the fly.

THE BRAZILIAN WANDERING SPIDER

Here's an impressive spider you will definitely want to avoid getting close to on your trip to the Amazon rainforest. The Brazilian Wandering

Spider is recorded as being the single most venomous spider in the world.

So, how bad would you feel if bitten? Well, the usual symptoms, which appear within half an hour of a bite, are crazy heartbeats, too high (or too low) blood pressure, stomach cramps, nausea, and dizziness. *Pretty scary stuff, right?* Luckily, this armed-and-ready fighter is most active at night and tends to sleep through the day in dark nooks. Plus, it always gives you a warning before lunging.

When threatened, it will stand on its hind legs and stick its front legs up in the air as if it's ready for a boxing fight!

FUN FACT: The Brazilian Wandering Spider is both the name of a single species and a whole family of what's called *armed spiders.* All up, over one dozen species of Brazilian wandering spiders live in the Amazon!

THE SCORPION-TAILED SPIDER

Another Australian beauty is the scorpion-tailed spider, a tiny critter that looks menacing but is mostly harmless. This spider boasts a scorpion tail (*that it curls up when it gets annoyed*) and boasts a gorgeous light brown color that makes it easily camouflage in the wild. Its biggest defense tactic is actually its color. During the day, when it lays motionless on grass or a branch, it looks like a dead leaf!

This very itsy-bitsy spider weighs only a fraction of an ounce and is just one inch in length. They prefer to live closer to the ground, which is why their webs are mostly found at ground level in gardens, parks, and forests. Amazingly, only females have the barbs at the end of their bodies.

FUN FACT: In total, there are about 12 species of scorpion-tailed spiders found in Australia, Asia, and Africa. New species are constantly discovered, and many scientists believe that this spider's camouflage tactic is **SO** good even researchers miss spotting them!

THE WOLF SPIDER

Wolf spiders are found throughout the world, and they would have to be among the most intimidating-looking spiders ever. *Truth be told, the name also doesn't help, right?* The Wolf is one of several spiders that actively hunt down prey rather than weave a web. It also uses clever antics like covering its nest entrance with organic waste in the hope of attracting insects. Once the insects arrive to devour what they think is a free lunch, **BAM**, *they become lunch!*

Recognizable due to its two oversized eyes (*it has eight in total, of course*), the Wolf Spider is a fast and capable hunter indeed. One of the few spiders with impeccable eyesight (*a rarity in the spider world*), the wolf can spot its prey from a great distance.

Wolf spiders are one of the species known to carry their babies with them on their backs, supporting them until they are large enough to go about the world on their own. *Such sweet mamas, right?*

FUN FACT: This spider is not aggressive towards humans, and by now, you will have learned that *none* of them are. No spider attacks without being provoked, and it is more likely to scuttle away from humans than run towards them. Given our colossal size difference, it makes a lot of sense: a spider is always more afraid of us than we should ever be of them!

THE JUMPING SPIDER

Jumping spiders are known for their incredible ability to make great leaps ahead. *The name kind of gave them away, right?* Just how far one can jump depends on the species, but, generally, every jumping spider can easily cover a distance that's 50 times their body length.

That's pretty impressive, don't you think?

Jumping spiders don't have special leg muscles that help them make huge leaps. Instead, when they want to jump, they redirect almost their entire blood flow to their hind legs, so they become bigger and more powerful. Then they propel themselves upwards at amazing speeds!

Aside from hunting its lunch, jumping spiders also use their bouncing ability to quickly escape predators, and that's a pretty neat defense trick.

Jumping spiders are the largest genus in the spider family. Almost 15% of all spiders are, in fact, jumping spiders.

FUN FACT: Jumping spiders are known for performing dance rituals to attract a mate. *They've got the moves!* Aside from swaying their front legs in the air (*like they just don't care*), they also do a totally neat tap-dancing routine. Except that they tap **SO** fast that it is not even visible to the human eye. Scientists need special cameras to catch the nifty dancers in action!

The kingdom of spiders is one of the most fascinating and least known in the animal world. Yet discovering cool facts about them can help us all love them a little more and fear them a little less.

For reasons even scientists don't fully understand, the fear of spiders (called **arachnophobia**) is the most common phobia in the world. *What is a phobia, you wonder?* A phobia is an uncontrollable and irrational fear. This means a person with a phobia can't help but feel fear, even if they know it makes no sense to be fearful of something.

And so, it is with spiders – amazing and helpful creatures that, for years, were believed to carry awful diseases. **By now, we know this isn't true!** We also know that spiders are not *really* deadly – not even the most venomous ones. We have developed antidotes and medication to treat bites, and dare we say, more people die in horseback riding accidents every year than they do from spider bites. *Yet we don't have an irrational fear of horses now, do we?*

Luckily, spiders also have an abundance of fans around the round. So many scientists are dedicating their lives to studying spiders, called **arachnology**.

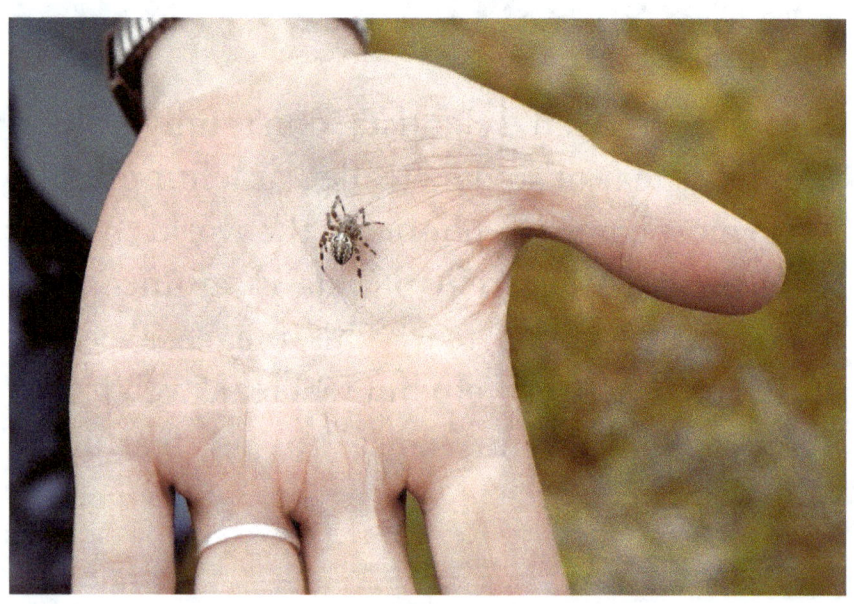

WHAT DO YOU CALL A SPIDER WITH 8 EYES?

A Spiiiiiiiiider!

THE FASCINATING HISTORY OF SPIDERS

Science suggests that all living creatures came from the sea. That once upon a time, we were all swimming creatures before *some* decided to take their first step on land.

Spiders were among the very first animals to live on land, and the most known ancestor of the modern-day spider lived in what's known as the **Devonian period**, some 380 million years ago. *That's about 150 million years before the first dinosaurs appeared on our planet!*

The ancestor of spiders had a much thinner waist than spiders today, yet it seems it could already weave a silky web. Early spiders were known to live on the ground and were preying on early arthropods such as giant silverfish, cockroaches, and millipedes. Spider webs, at this point, were just known to serve as protection for their eggs. Scientists believe spiders started to use their webs to catch prey around 250 million years ago.

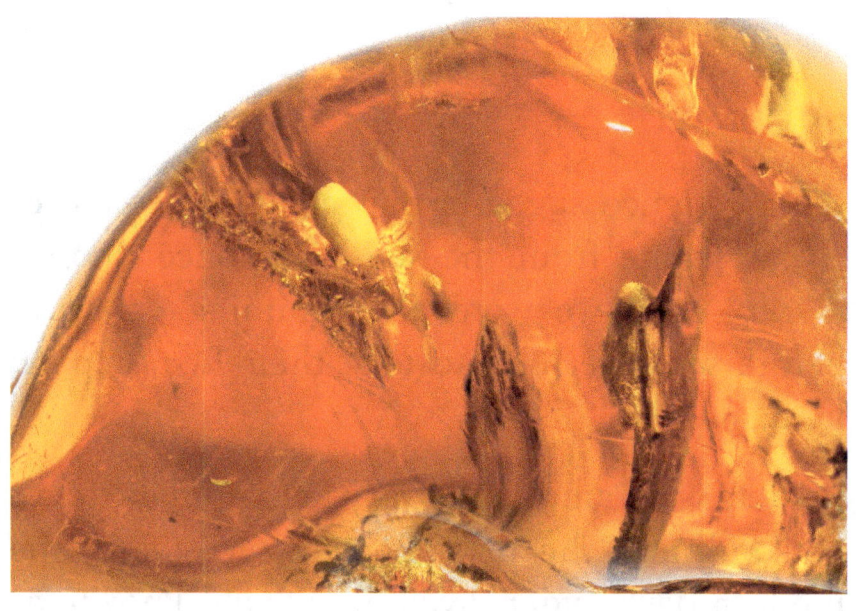

Later on, in the **Jurassic period** (*yes, when dinosaurs started to roam the planet!*), spiders and their web use also evolved. As time passed, they became better at weaving larger webs to catch their meals. It was around this time that spiders evolved the ability to weave webs in the air and spin them into orbs.

ARE SPIDERS RELATED TO ANY OTHER ANIMAL ON EARTH?

As it turns out, **the horseshoe crab** is one of the spider's closest relatives. These are some bizarre-looking creatures! They do not look like horseshoes, and they most definitely do *not* look like crabs. Yet they are arachnids like spiders and scorpions. Scientists proved that they are relatives of spiders when they studied their DNA. Based on fossil records, horseshoe crabs' ancestors lived around the same time the ancestors of arachnids did, about 450 million years ago.

It just so happened that the horseshoe crabs stayed underwater while spiders went on to live mostly on land. Both are super tough to have survived many extinction events like the ones that wiped out dinosaurs.

WHAT DO YOU CALL IT WHEN YOU HAVE TOO MANY SPIDERS IN YOUR HOUSE?

A no-fly zone!

WHERE DO SPIDERS LIKE TO LIVE?

Spiders are one of the most widespread creatures in the world, and as we now know, they don't like very cold places, nor do they live on top of very high mountains. They live in both tropical and temperate climates and are found on wetlands, swamps, bogs, and marshes.

These clever animals are highly adaptable in all sorts of habitats, like deserts, rainforests, and mountains. This is because they are such skilled hunters and trappers. As long as there are plenty of insects and creepy crawlies to feast on, a spider will thrive quite well almost anywhere.

Have you ever wondered if spiders travel? As a matter of fact, they do! Spiders are good travelers, and they will transfer habitats if they need to. The cobwebs that spiders leave behind when they move on can easily be considered Mother Nature's architecture. You could say that spiders are superb designers *and* decorators, building their own homes, nesting grounds, and traps.

I ONLY WANTED TO HUG YOU...

WITH ALL 8 OF MY ARMS!

UNIQUE CHARACTERISTICS AND APPEARANCE OF SPIDERS

Since there are so many spider species the world over, you can imagine how different the many characteristics distinct species boast. So, first up: *what do they all have in common?*

EYESIGHT:

Most spider species have eight eyes, yet a few have only six. Very few, however, have good eyesight. Instead, the spider relies on sound and vibration to navigate toward its prey. *Why is that so?* Because most spiders are actually **nocturnal**, which means they hunt during the night (when it is dark, anyhow) and sleep during the day. It is no surprise, therefore, that the spiders with the sharpest eyesight are **diurnal** species or species that hunt during the day. You can also guess which spider has good vision by learning about its hunting technique. If a spider weaves a web and waits for prey to land on it, it will use vibration and sound more than sight. If, however, it hunts and jumps, then you know it must *see* the prey, first and foremost!

LEGS:

Spiders are nimble and fast on the ground. *How could they not?* Spiders have 8 jointed legs, which means they also have 48 knees! It's the hairs on a spider's legs that help the animal detect vibrations from passing prey.

DIET:

A spider's diet includes mosquitoes, moths, and flies, yet many spiders also chow down on much bigger prey like mice and, in some cases, even fellow spiders. **Oops.** Guess when the appetite pangs hit, anything's a meal! Spiders eat about 10% of their body weight per day. Although most are carnivorous (*they eat only other animals*), a few are vegetarian, preferring to feast on plants instead.

EATING:

The way spiders devour their meal is rather unique. Spiders can't actually chew or swallow food as we do, or other animals do. Instead, once they capture their prey, they inject them with venom through their fangs and turn their insides into liquid goop. **Yikes!** Then, they start sucking them to consume them like juice.

BALLOONING:

By far the coolest of all spider superpowers, ballooning is how spiders can travel great distances. As the name suggests, the spider creates a balloon of silken threads, which it then uses to catch the wind and take flight. Baby spiders (called **spiderlings**) use this technique when they finally emerge from their woven sack. Unfortunately, ballooning (*also known as kiting because it's like flying a kite!*) is not very controllable. The spider is at the mercy of the wind currents, which means it can easily fly in the wrong direction or straight into a predator. Nevertheless, it is still an amazing characteristic!

THE SPIDER'S WEB

Even though not all spiders weave webs, it remains the most iconic of all spider characteristics. All over the world, this is what spiders are most known for!

A spider's web starts off as a silk liquid inside the abdomen and is secreted through the spinnerets. Once the liquid comes in contact with air, it becomes solid. **Essentially, it becomes a thread!** A spider will use its spinning tools (*the spinnerets*) to start weaving an elaborate web from this thread.

Spiders have a lot of uses for their webs. They use them to protect their eggs before the spiderlings hatch, to travel, and hunt for food. Contrary to popular belief, spider webs do not trap insects but rather attract them. They are very shiny for a good reason: to reflect UV light so it will be more attractive to their targets.

Spiders weave large webs and replace them daily, making them not just hard workers but very meticulous builders too. It takes a spider about an hour to spin a complete web. Amazingly, spiders can produce different kinds of silk, depending on their use. *A web to catch insects, for example, will be sticky, while a ballooning web will be sturdy!*

FUN FACT: The silk strand of a spider's web is about five times stronger than steel of the same size!

THE SPIDERS' VENOM

Not all spiders release venom upon biting, but most do. The venom's role is to weaken the prey, not kill it. This is why spider venom is not as dangerous to humans as many believe, given we are much bigger animals than their intended prey. Once the prey is weak and can no longer fight back, the spider will then kill and eat it. And such is the circle of animal life.

Spiders also use their venom to defend themselves when predators threaten them, which is why humans are sometimes accidentally bitten. The spider knows we are not prey, but it is its way of telling us to back right off.

WHAT DO YOU CALL TWO SPIDERS WHO JUST GOT MARRIED?

Newlywebs!

THE LIFE CYCLE OF SPIDERS

The life cycle of a spider consists of three stages: the **egg**, **spiderling**, and **adult** phases. Depending on the species, spiders can lay up to 3,000 eggs in one or more sacs made of silk.

Eggs usually hatch after two to three weeks.

Mama spiders keep their eggs safe by keeping them in nests made of the super-strong silk-like sac. Male spiders usually die after making babies with female spiders, which is not all that unusual. Many insects are known for this exact characteristic. After mating, the male will die so the female can eat him and thus get the nourishment she needs to raise her babies. *It's a form of sacrifice that's meant to keep the species thriving!*

In some species, even the female dies after laying eggs.

The next stage, right after the eggs hatch, is the **spiderling** stage. Most spiderlings will stay close to where they were hatched until they can explore their territory. As mentioned, spiderlings can already utilize ballooning and go to certain parts of their habitat, some going to very high places or really far from where they were conceived.

Spiderlings, given their soft bodies, are very vulnerable at this point. As they grow, they will molt and molt until they have a solid and strong exoskeleton for support and protection.

Spiderlings will molt about five to ten times before turning into **full-grown adults**. Take note that female spiders are always larger than male ones, and so they reach adulthood much later. A male spider usually only lives for two years, but it varies from species to species. Female spiders generally live longer.

Jumping spider molt

Tarantulas live an unusually long life compared to non-tarantula species. *They can live for up to a whopping 20 years!*

THANK YOU FOR READING

Spiders are among the cleverest and most helpful animals on the planet. We owe them a lot of gratitude for all the hard work they do, keeping our homes, gardens, farms, and forests in perfect natural balance. Without spiders, our planet would be overrun with pests and our crops destroyed. **Without spiders in the world, we could not grow enough food to eat!**

Understandably, however, many families are a little wary of having *too* many spiders in their homes. Luckily, there are many ways to deter spiders from homes and gardens without causing them harm.

Do you have someone in your life who is afraid of spiders? Why don't you share some of the spider love and facts with them and help them understand spiders a little better? **Most of the time, we are simply scared of what we don't know!**

It is important to understand that spiders play a critical role in the balance of our ecosystem, and their wild habitat, the forests, and grasslands, must be maintained for their (*and our*) protection. The best way to help protect spiders is by protecting their habitats. Good environmental practices, like recycling, avoiding single-use plastic, and not polluting waterways, go a long way in ensuring a healthier planet for spiders and all the animals on our planet.

LET'S HANG OUT!

THANK YOU!

T hank you for reading this book and for allowing us to share our love for spiders with you!

If you've enjoyed this book, please let us know by leaving a rating and a brief review wherever you made your purchase! This helps us spread the word to other readers!

Thank you for your time, and have an awesome day!

For more information, please visit:

www.animalreads.com

© Copyright 2022 - All rights reserved Admore Publishing

ISBN: 978-3-96772-117-1

ISBN: 978-3-96772-118-8

Animal Reads at www.animalreads.com

The content contained within this book may not be reproduced, duplicated or transmitted without direct written permission from the author or the publisher.

Under no circumstances will any blame or legal responsibility be held against the publisher, or author, for any damages, reparation, or monetary loss due to the information contained within this book. Either directly or indirectly.

Published by Admore Publishing: Gotenstraße, Berlin, Germany

www.admorepublishing.com

www.ingramcontent.com/pod-product-compliance
Lightning Source LLC
LaVergne TN
LVHW020143080526
838202LV00048B/3993